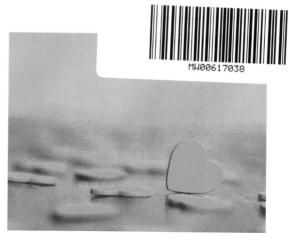

# Two as One Forever

## *A Better You, A Better Marriage*

### Beverly V. Thomas

ISBN 978-1-63961-929-0 (paperback)
ISBN 978-1-63961-930-6 (digital)

Christian Faith Publishing
832 Park Avenue
Meadville, PA 16335
www.christianfaithpublishing.com

Printed in the United States of America

Eddie and Beverly's Remarriage (1998)

I dedicate this book to my wonderful husband—the one person in this life that has endured all my faults, inhibitions, and dysfunctions. Knowing I have a best friend that doesn't judge me but always wants to help me. A friend that I know loves me for who I am.

We were given a second chance, just as God gives us all, over and over and over. The road wasn't easy, and there were many ups and downs. But we trusted and sustained far past self, looking beyond our own reserves and embracing the courage to withstand the trials of life, managing to stand strong and push through, and accepting the Lord to be first in *all* aspects of our lives. Resting in Him is the best we could have done for our marriage.

So, I say, thank you, babe, for the journey. We made it!

I can do all things through Christ which strengtheneth me.

—Philippians 4:13

# Contents

# Foreword

At a recent convention luncheon, my husband, Cal, and I were seated with four other couples we did not know. The couple to our left began a conversation with us. They revealed that they had been married twelve years. Seeing that they looked to be in their sixties, I knew there had to be a back story. The husband shared that they each had been widowed and that between their current marriage and each of their former marriages, they had eighty-one years between them. The wife didn't say much, but she very passionately declared that each time she attends a wedding ceremony, and the officiant gets to the "till death do us part" portion of the vows, she wants to jump up and ask, "Do you really understand what that vow means?" This couple obviously knows the meaning of that professed promise—so does Beverly Thomas.

I've never been asked to write the foreword for a book until Beverly asked me to write one for her. I can happily do it because I can unreservedly endorse its author. Cal and I have the wonderful privilege of pastoring a church in which three divorced couples have been reunited in marriage to their respective spouses after years of being divorced. Beverly and Eddie Thomas are one of these couples.

The biblical principles contained in these pages are the hard-fought truths that Beverly stood on while God worked in her and Eddie to bring their broken marriage to a place of healing and restoration. Writing is hard, but Beverly took it on as a labor of love so that she could use her pain as medicine for you, dear reader. This journey to wholeness has also caused Beverly to leave her previous employment and use her experiences and giftings to help other couples as a marriage coach through the ministry she founded, 2 As1 Forever.

Beverly writes from a biblical worldview and believes that truth is found in the Bible, but truth alone cannot set you free. It's the truth you *know* (cf. John 8:32) and apply that will bring freedom. Truth is powerful and can change you! If you apply to your own life, the "worked out in the trenches" biblical wisdom that Beverly sets forth in this book, you, too, can experience health and healing in your marriage which is God's will for every marriage.

—Sandy Garcia
Auburn Hills Christian Center

# Grow in Your Marriage

Look beyond today and see the beauty in your marriage. Remain in hope, love, belief, and faith. Trust God for your spouse and your marriage. Your marriage will be that remarkable journey in life that will humble you to a place of selflessness. The ability to always have a giving heart without any expectations of a return will place you in an indescribable and unimaginable joy of the Lord.

It takes courage to trust and forgive. Happiness comes from within, not another person. Even though the journey may feel lonely at times, know you are never alone.

# *Inspired by Life*

This book was inspired by personal testimony. A divorce and remarriage to the same man was an unexpected turn in life. Forcing me to see the attempts of making my own plans for life here on this earth was not the design intended for me.

When I heard God speak, *That's your husband*, it became clear that what He joined together, no man can separate. That was a life alteration for me and the realization of what we do is to be for His purpose and not our own.

He taught me to put Him first and not to look back; to move forward trusting in Him with everything concerning all things, especially my marriage. Therefore, when the trials come, and they will come, I look to God to overcome the challenges that this world brings.

It's been an amazing journey. I've learned the depth of "oneness." Moving past myself and loving a man unconditionally is where God needed me to be. I must admit, I'm still learning and still growing.

Due to the obedience to God and His Word, I find myself with joy, peace, and belief in knowing He will never leave me nor forsake me, as He said. It isn't about the start nor the finish. It's all about the journey.

I thank God for my husband, Eddie, and the life He chose for me. I will be forever grateful for His love toward me.

Remain in peace!

The journey of marriage is both critical and interesting. At some point, all the happiness and blissful experiences tend to disappear at the glimpse of challenges. But without any controversy, the miracle of marriage is one of the greatest. God, at His own discretion, created a perfect union such that two become one according to the holy ordinance.

It is such a glorious bond that should not be taken as an easy task. It is meant to be worked upon. Marriage is a sensitive and fragile institution that must be nurtured and protected if they are to survive for a lifetime. It is an exciting and eventful type of change. Going from an independent individual to being accountable for someone else's needs, wants, and wishes requires an enormous paradigm shift in thinking.

The Bible tells us that "two are better than one, because they have a pleasant reward for their hard work. For if one among them should fall, the other one can raise his partner up. But how will it be with just the person who falls when there is not another to raise him up" (Ecclesiastes 4:9–10 NIV).

God is the only wise God, and in His infinite wisdom, He has instituted marriage. As a result, it takes only the wisdom that comes from God to sustain marriage and make it count. Following godly counsels and principles in marriage is absolutely important if a marriage is to succeed. In this book, I will take you through some life-transforming counsels and principles that have helped not just my marriage but many other marriages.

Everyone desires a blissful marriage; however, it does not happen automatically. There is always a price to pay. If you truly want to succeed in marriage, you must first be willing to work on yourself to become a better person in all aspects of life, particularly, as it has to do with marriage.

# What Is Marriage?

The vocation to marriage may be very stunning, and it's primarily based on love. On the grounds that God is love, and He created the arena out of affection, He desired children to be born inside the love that males and females commit to each other for his or her complete lifestyles. Through marriage, male and female emerge as collaborators with God, particularly when children arrive. The spouses are known as to sanctify each other. At the same time, they receive the project of forming and educating the heartfelt love, intelligence, and will of their children until the day they may be self-sustaining and responsible.

Marriage is a state of being joined to a person of the opposite sex (only) as husband and wife.

It is a legal or religious ceremony that formalizes the decision of a man and a woman to live as husband and wife.

It is the social institution under which man and woman establish their decision to live as husband and wife by a legal commitment and religious ceremony.

It is the foundational element of all human society; it is also the foundation upon which the church as God's special society rests.

A Christian marriage is more than just the union of two Christians of the opposite sex. It is characterized and governed by Christian principles that are taught in the Bible. They are to enjoy the company of each other for life. They must keep to their vows, which are in sickness and in health, for better or worse. The minister now pronounces them husband and wife.

The bride and groom look lovingly into each other's eyes. Family, friends, and even casual acquaintances cheer them on. Two people have found each other a lifetime of commitment, vowed to be devoted and loving, and promised never to leave or forsake each other.

Vows of faithfulness are the core of marriage. Through those vows, two people, in a miraculous way, become one. Then they begin a lifetime of doing things together, like solving problems together.

God approves of marriage in general. In fact, He instituted it by Himself. The family is a bedrock of the society, and marriage is the foundation of the family.

If we want to live the way God designed us to, pleasing Him and making things easier for ourselves, we must know God's teaching on marriage.

The Bible tells us, "The Lord God said, 'It is not good that the man should be alone, I will make him a help meet for him'" (Genesis 2:18).

Mark 10:7–9 explains why a man leaves his father and his mother and is joined to his wife, and the two become one.

Marriage was God's idea from the very beginning. It is as old as Eden and yet as fresh as the last wedding. Marriage is ordained by God, a sacred relationship, one not to be entered lightly.

The distinction between an ordinary marriage and an extraordinary marriage is in giving just a "little more" every day, as often as possible, for as long as you both shall be together.

God intends each of our marriages to be a way for us to be totally fulfilled, but we have to live as an example of Christ's love for us. As sweet as marriage is, let us understand that real life is filled with distractions. Even if they are worthy distractions, you still need to focus and be motivated to take action in your marriage.

In this book, we will critically consider the important factors that influence marriage. Some factors influence marriage positively while others do negatively. It is the will of God for every marriage to succeed. Separation is never the will of God for any marriage.

It is easy to think that only "others" get separated and that your own marriage is somehow immune to divorce. As a result, you think only others encounter infidelity and contend over who receives the house, the car, the pet. Besides, how many of us would walk down the aisle if we knew our relationships would terminate in the court for divorce?

Sincerely, no relationship comes with a lifetime assurance. Even men and women who are raised in stable homes are vulnerable. In addition, those who go to church and call themselves Christians, who vow "until death separates us," can still fall into troubles.

Is marriage perfect? Will we ever get it right? Dr. Myles Munroe put it this way: "Marriage is bigger than the two people in it. Because marriage is a perfect vow made before a perfect God by two imperfect people, only God can make it work." He reminds us to go to the source for guidance and direction even when it comes to marriage.

As Christians, we know that acting out biblical principles to marriage will give us a more solid foundation than those of our unbelieving relatives and neighbors. Certainly, we know this. But what are we doing about it? In other words, what makes a marriage "Christian"?

# It Begins with Love

The importance of love in marriage cannot be overemphasized as it is the engine room of oneness in marriage. Every activity in marriage must be done within the confines of love. Love is such a great thing, especially when it is true. Any marriage that is built within the domain of true love will succeed.

This love must be known, understood, and applied for a marriage to be successful.

God gives us a definition of love in 1 Corinthians 13. As you go through these verses, realize that godly love is not just a warm affection for someone. The Bible tells us:

> Love is patient, love is kind. It does not envy, it does not brag, it has no pride. It is not rude, it is not selfish, it is not easily annoyed, it counts no wrongs. Love does not rejoice in evil but delight in truth. It protects, always trusts, always hope, always endures. Love never disappoints.
> (1 Corinthians 13:4–8a)

This adds a new perspective on the concept of the words "I love you." Pause to consider what this type of love looks like. Honey, I love you. What I mean is that I am patient and kind to you. I am not envious of you. I do not brag in front of you. I am not proud in front of you. I am not offensive to you. I seek your good and not my own. I am not easily angered by you, and I keep no record of your wrongs. Wow! If only we can live this way all the time!

If we are truthful, however, most of us will agree that this kind of love is not as easy as it sounds. Some of the reason for this is that we find it less difficult to be selfish than to be selfless. It is much easier for us to think of ourselves and our needs instead of the needs of the people around us. When we live our lives in this manner, however, those close to us do not feel as though we sincerely love them. This is true when it has to do with our spouses.

One of the major characteristics of godly love, however, is that it is focused more upon others than upon us. Did you take note of verse 5 above? It says that love "is not self-seeking." Indeed, Jesus said in the Bible, "Greater love has no one than this: that he lay down his life for his friends" (John 15:13). Of course, this is exactly the type of love that Jesus showed for us! And this is the type of love that concentrates on need to show to our spouses as well.

When we first fall in love, we normally say things like "I love you" or "I want to be with you." The point is on the *I* side of the equation. This is okay and good. But true love in a healthy marriage concentrates on meeting the desires of our spouse and not our own selfish desires.

Falling in love is only the starting point. It's the first step in a thrilling journey where two persons become united. But the extreme feelings of intimacy felt at first will fade off.

We know that love and infatuation are not the same. We also know that love isn't just a feeling. Love is a commitment. It's a deliberate action of choosing to dedicate one's whole life to making your loved one preferred.

If your love is founded upon emotions alone, then your marriage will fail. The focus should be on sustaining the union and cultivating an appreciation for one another daily. This leads to harmony and warmth. And you will begin experiencing firsthand what it truly means to tenderly nurture each other.

It is for this very reason that marriage advice typically centers on the idea of being considerate toward one's partner. Otherwise, selfishness creeps in and chokes the relationship.

Love is more than an emotion; it's a verb—an action that we demonstrate continually regardless of how we happen to feel on any given day.

How selfless is your love? What would your spouse say about the selflessness of your love? Are you more interested in what you can get out of the relationship or in what you can put into the relationship?

Loving your spouse selflessly and unselfishly creates true love in marriage.

Scripturally speaking, marriage is defined as the union of a man and woman who make a covenant before God to fulfil their God-given duties to one another in marriage. One of the obligations God calls them to is to have marital love toward each another. The scriptural kind of love is highly sacrificial in nature. It requires willingness and deliberate acts to ensure its sustainability. Before we go deeper into this journey, let us briefly point out some acts that characterize the true (agape) love.

Scriptural agape love in marriage is

- GIVING my body to my spouse to satisfy their sexual desires.
- PATIENCE toward my spouse concerning their faults.
- KINDNESS to my spouse both in words and deeds. It is kindness in taking care of the physical needs of my spouse whether it's taking care of them when they are sick, making sure they are well fed, or satisfying their sexual desires.
- SACRIFICING my own health for my spouse's well-being.
- HONORING my spouse's God-given gender role in our union together.
- FORGIVING my spouse for the sin they committed against me.
- BEING TRUTHFUL with my spouse. This doesn't mean **brutal** honesty—you know the old line "Do I look fat in this outfit?" It does not mean we must say out loud every thought that enters our mind or how we feel about every situation in the moment.

But what it means is not telling lies to hide our sin from each other. It also means that sometimes we must do as the Bible says and "say the truth in love" to each other when we believe they are acting unlawfully, as love does not rejoice in iniquity.

- **PROTECTING** each other's personality and dignity.
- **TRUSTING** that my spouse desires the best interests, and without evidence to the contrary, believing what my spouse says to me about events that may have happened.
- **HOPING** in my spouse's capacity even when they seem too deficient in some areas. It always hopes that they will succeed or that they will be better. This is a type of hope that encourages our spouses in whatever they set their mind to accomplish.
- **ENDURING** through arguments or quarrels, health issues, and physical changes in my own or my spouse's body. It endures loss of job, economic status changes, or changes in residence.
- **CONSTANT**, because it is based on a deliberate life choice and not upon my emotions toward my spouse at any given moment.

True love, sacred love, love of the soul does
not inhabit the heart of the unbeliever.

—George Sand, *Mademoiselle La Quintinie* (1863)

Everyone who wants to succeed in marriage must develop the capacity to walk in love the right way. As we continue in this journey, you will receive a life-transforming understanding that will help you develop the capacity to make your marriage a better one.

For a holistic understanding, I will take us through the different types of love.

## Types of Love

*Love,* as a word, gets thrown around a lot these days and applied to all sorts of types of relationships and emotions. But in the New Testament of the Bible, written in Greek, the authors used more specific terms to describe different types of love.

Sexual love (eros)—This kind of love is based on sexual attraction. It is the first driving force for most men looking for a woman to be joined in marriage. A woman may be attracted sexually to a man also before marriage, or she may grow to be sexually attracted to him after marriage. The scripture has an entire book dedicated to this kind of love, the Songs of Solomon.

Friendship love (phileo)—This kind of love is based on either romantic emotion between a man and woman, feelings of infatuation, or love that is anchored on common interests. This kind of love is close to 100 percent based on how much each individual put into the relationship, whether it is a same-sex friendship, a dating relationship, or a marriage union.

Choice love (agape)—This kind of love is not based on feelings toward one's spouse, and it is not based on sexual attraction toward one's spouse. Instead, it is based on the choice a person made when they entered into the covenant of marriage with each other. In choosing to enter into this covenant, they have committed to performing some actions toward their spouse irrespective of their feelings or sexual desires at any given time in the future. This is often why, in additional to calling agape a "choice love," it's also a "commitment love" and an "action love."

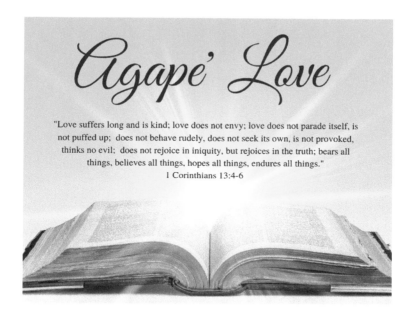

In the context of marriage, once you made your wedding vows and vowed to love your spouse in good times and in bad, in sickness and health, till death does one part, you were vowing to like them with agape love (choice love, aside from feelings). You almost certainly were motivated to vow Agape love to them out of the philia love you had which is predicated on feelings of friendship and romance.

Philia love isn't bad, but it can become bad if that's the sole foundation for a wedding, for it will not always be there. It comes and goes. But agape is usually there because it's not supported by feelings but on a commitment made to God.

So what distinguishes marital love from other sorts of love?

If you were to notice the different attributes of affection I gave, especially those supported in the First Epistle of Paul the Apostle to the Corinthians 13:4–8, you'll easily see that a lot of those attributes apply to other relationships besides marriage. They might apply to friendships or maybe the parent-child relationship. But here I'm trying to use First Epistle of Paul the Apostle to the Corinthians 13:4–8, a passage not specifically about marital love but to marriage because God involves agape love in our marriage. The Bible tells us:

> Hearing that Jesus had quieted the Sadducees, the Pharisees got together. One among them, an expert within the law, tested him with this question:

"Teacher, which is that the greatest
commandment within the Laws?" Jesus
answered: "Love the Lord your God with
all of your heart and with all of your soul
and with your entire mind. This is often
the primary and greatest commandment.
And therefore the second is like it: Love
your neighbour as yourself. All the Law
and therefore the Prophets hang on these
two commandments." (Matthew 22:34–
40 NIV)

The reason I mention Matthew 22 is because the concept of a person loving his wife as he loves himself isn't new
or maybe exclusive to marital love. As Christians, we are to
like all people around us as we love ourselves.

The key to understanding the uniqueness of marital
love is seen in Ephesians 5:29, "For no man ever yet dislikes
his own body; but nourished and cherished it, as the Lord
the church."

There are two keywords in verse 29 that help us begin
to differentiate the love God wants between a husband and
wife. The Greek word *ektrepho* interpreted in English as
*nourish* in this verse has got to do with "feeding to bring back
maturity." The second Greek word *thalpo* translated as *cherished* originally mentioned a mother bird "keeping warm" her
eggs as she sat up on them. This Greek word later came to
mean "tender care," but it's an equivalent idea.

So, in essence, Ephesians 5:29 is telling us that even
as a mother bird warms her eggs then feeds her babies and
brings them to maturity, this is often like what Christ does
for his church in caring for her physical and spiritual needs
and bringing her to maturity.

When taken within the complete context of Ephesians 5, even as Christ brings the church to spiritual maturity and tenderly care for her spiritual and physical needs, so do husbands need to worry for the physical and spiritual needs of their wives and convey them to spiritual maturity.

But this is often only the primary part of the distinctiveness of marital love found in Ephesians 5, the foremost profound distinctive characteristic of marital love is found in verse 31. The Bible tells us in Ephesians 31, "For this cause shall a person leave his father and mother, and shall be joined unto his wife, and that they two shall be one flesh."

The physical union of a person to his wife, the coupling, is what marks the most peculiarity of marital love. This is often why sex is mentioned as "the act of marriage."

In marriage, a man and woman should be joined on all three levels—spirit, emotion, and body.

Now all believers and even many nonbelievers would accept as true the statement I just said above about the necessity for a husband and wife to be united on these levels in marriage. But the disagreement comes in *how* a man and woman are to be united in these three ways.

Let me also drop a bit of understanding on how a man and woman can truly be united in marriage.

We see it all the time among engaged or married couples. They appear to be so united and in sync with each other. They often finish each other's sentences and that they rarely, if ever, fight. Except for anyone who has been married for an extended length of time, we will all tell you that the unity of marriage when the connection is new is predicated on one thing and one thing alone, folks—good old-fashioned hormones.

It is quite humorous to ascertain this with newlyweds. Most times, newlyweds are insistent that their unity will never change, which it'll be exactly because it is when their marriage is new for the remainder of the wedding. I even have to hold back the chuckles whenever I hear a newlywed couple say this with such sincerity in their hearts. I said this before and I will say it again—new love between a man and a woman is an emotionally and hormonally-driven love that produces a kind of temporary insanity especially in men.

After a time, whether it's six months or a year, this hormonally-based love eventually comes to an end; therefore, the real mature and long-lasting love in marriage can be built which will stand the test of time.

The Bible however presents a way during which a husband and a wife are to become one in marriage. The Bible tells us:

> For the husband is that the head of the wife, as Christ is that the head of the church: and he's the saviour of the body. Therefore because the church is subject unto Christ, so let the wives be to their own husbands in everything. (Ephesians 5:23–24 KJV)

In scriptural marriage, the way a man and woman become one is that same way the church becomes one with Christ. He leads and she follows. As Church is molding itself round the wishes and leadership of Christ, so, too, a wife is to mold herself to the needs and leading of her husband.

The Bible teaches that conformity is the key to oneness in marriage. In Christian marriage, the man conforms his will to God's will; therefore, the wife conforms her will to her own husband's will in love.

Sadly, so many Christian marriages this day are built on negative compromise instead of conformity; therefore, the truth is that men and women are equally responsible for this sad state of affairs. Women are responsible because they emotionally badger their husbands into compromising with them on important affairs of the house even when he believes God would have their family do things differently. Men, on the opposite hand, are responsible for not standing up as men of God and selecting to evolve to the desire of God instead of compromising what they know to be right because of peace with their wedded wives.

I am not implying that a husband cannot listen to advice from his spouse and adhere to it. Or that marriage removes a woman's unique identity because it doesn't. God made all individuals unique, and he even made all of his local churches unique. No two individuals or two churches are exactly alike. But when it involves the important matters of life especially within the areas of religion, child-rearing, teaching, and finances, a wife is to mold herself to the pattern of her husband. However, there is a positive way of compromise which we will consider later in this book, but every conformity and compromise must be within the proportion of faith.

We have seen how that is; biblical marital love is distinct from all other loves therein it calls on a husband and wife to model their love for each other after the love that exists between Christ and his church. The wife totally depends upon her husband for her nourishment and protection in the same way that the Church places her dependence on Christ for her nourishment and protection.

The husband should look after the spiritual and physical needs of his wife and tenderly look after and protect her the way Christ does to the Church.

The husband and wife should roll in the hay regularly, and sometimes, not only to satisfy one another's physical needs and avoid temptation, but they need to also realize that their physical union in sex is the most distinctive and most defining act of marital love.

One last note I would like to feature here about sexuality in marriage. A little like all of the opposite points of marital love, sexual relations in marriage should never be dependent upon feelings at any given time. The Bible is crystal clear that they are to come together sexually, regularly, apart for a brief time by mutual consent.

While it's nice to try to do things for our spouse (whether it's husbands for wives or wives for husbands), sex in marriage should never *ever* need to be earned. The moment a husband and wife say "I do," it becomes implemented.

This is not always a husband-desiring-from-a-wife thing either. I do know of a new marriage, a young couple, where the husband would rather play video games or do things together with his friends than to "roll in the hay" with his wife, and this should never be the case. The Bible sees sex as the distinctive symbol of the wedding relationship.

As has been established earlier on, the journey of marriage is characterized by life challenges that will always want to tear the wedding apart. But you must fight against every challenge with the weapon of faith and love. We have considered the subject of love, but love cannot work outside the faith. This is because while walking in love, there will be challenges, and challenges are overcome by faith.

The Bible tells us in 1 John 5:4, "And this is often the victory that overcomes the world, even our faith."

It is faith that brought us to God, and it is the same faith that keeps and sustains us in God. Because faith honors God, God also honors faith. Whenever we turn to God or cry to Him, He responds to us on the basis of our faith. It's an act of putting God first and giving Him the pre-eminence.

If faith guarantees God's intervention in our marriage, then we will boldly say that faith guarantees success in marriage.

Let's face it. The scripture teaches us not to be "unequally yoked" (2 Corinthians 6:14). It means that your common denominator should be a relationship with Jesus. Many dating and engaged couples have not realized how important this is until they face the challenges of marriage and then they hit a wall with conflict after conflict after conflict.

You need the Lord Jesus. He is the glue to offer you the faith and therefore the strength to humble yourself and get through the challenges. When Jesus is put at the center of your marriage—in the great times and also the bad times—you experience a depth and richness that you simply couldn't have without Him.

The value of a spiritual connection is infinite and unimaginable. Moreover, it's vital during a healthy marriage. Yet many Christian couples desire that they have a deeper spiritual life together. It is very good to desire, but somehow, they really never get around to making it happen. Their intentions are good, but their excuses ("I don't have time for spiritual things," "My spouse isn't interested") easily override their purposes.

There are numerous homes—even Christian homes—where the spiritual connection is dead, and therefore the marriage is of course following. We discover numerous couples living in a daze, wondering what piece of their marriage puzzle is missing.

Every couple needs soul-to-soul closeness. If you would like to enjoy the deepest level of connection in marriage, you would want to develop spiritual intimacy in your relationship. There's nothing weird or mystical about spiritual intimacy. It's simply a wedding of three—an intimate relationship between God, a husband, and a wife. Profound intimacy happens when two hearts, two bodies, two souls connect with the God who created them and designed marriage.

There may be times in your marriage when you're driving down the freeway with one hand on the wheel and the other hand on your forehead, and you're thinking, *I can't take another step in my marriage. Nobody understands what I'm going through. This is often so big; I don't even think I'll survive.*

When you have faith in the Creator of the universe, then you'll survive. In fact, you'll even survive the losses, hurts, financial failures, and all the things that life brings. Your marriage is going to be richer for the trials; that is the role of faith in your marriage. Once you realize that you're not alone, you go to God and say, "Help me, God. Help me to understand what You would like me to do in this situation. Help me learn what You would like me to find out through this." Faith is total dependence on God.

Let me briefly take us through some ways faith can help us build a sustainable marriage that stands the test of time:

***Learn to pray for your spouse.*** Praying for the welfare of your partner and asking God to watch over her or him helps to sustain marriage. Praying for others makes for increased commitment and more satisfying relationships.

***You must be spiritually open and sincere.*** New parents who were ready to share their beliefs with their spouses in a way that enabled them to ascertain one another as "soul mates" are more likely to resolve conflicts in a positive manner. Greater spiritual intimacy provides couples with a spiritual resource to motivate them to stay kind and resist the urge to 'go negative' once they discuss their core conflicts. Spiritual connection appears to be one unique resource that inspire some spouses to preserve and protect their marriage as soon as they become married.

***You must be compassionate.*** On the opposite end of the generational scale, a study of sixty-four married older couples found that the assumption that marriage features a sacred character was associated with both increased marital satisfaction and compassionate love. Sacred beliefs regarding a wedding may inspire "the sort of love that gives motivation, encouragement, and context to prioritize the requirements of the spouse over the self" (Auburn University and East Carolina University).

***You must have an intimate relationship with God.*** A deep relationship with God provides you with the required power and ability to create the right atmosphere for forgiveness, love, and a strong support for your home. The inspiration that will help you build a successful marriage must come from God. Relationship with God opens you up to the spiritual resources that will strengthen you and prepare you for a glorious marriage experience.

***You must hold on to faith.*** Faith regulates your activities and restrains you from negative acts. The way you respond to offense from your spouse and other life challenges is a function of your faith. It grants you the capacity to make the right choice even in the midst of great trials and difficulties. In faith, you will always make the right determination that will strengthen and sustain your marriage for life. Faith provides you with a shield and protection from uncertainties; you will realize that you will less likely be a victim of evil circumstance or be part of evil doing.

If the spirit is willing, the flesh might not be so weak. Faith is much more than believing; it is an act. You must learn to practice the things you believe. If you set your mind to practice the things that are consistent with faith, then the success of your marriage is guaranteed.

Your faith toward God brings you into the domain of God's unlimited favor and grace to function effectively in marriage. Since marriage is divine, it takes divine ability to work it out. Anchoring your faith in God enables you to have great achievement far beyond your natural ability.

In faith, you will always do the right thing. This is because your choices, decisions, resolves, and actions are divinely inspired. If you must be victorious in marriage, faith is the guarantee, for we walk by faith and not by sight.

Let us, furthermore, look into another critical factor that makes for a successful marriage.

# The Freedom of Forgiveness

*Forgiveness*

...will allow the beauty of self to flourish.
Let go of the hurts from yesterday and
embrace the joys of today.
Move forward with a pure heart
and let Peace free you.

It is therefore very important for you to keep you heart open, even as we delve into this critical factor that makes for a successful marriage. An unforgiving spirit is absolutely detrimental to the success of marriage. As you keep your heart open, God of all grace will change you from inside out. He will equip you with the strength, capacity, and the grace for forgiveness.

Forgiveness within the Bible is a "release" or a "dismissal" of something. The forgiveness we have in Christ involves the discharge of sinners from God's just penalty and therefore the complete release of all charges against us (see Romans 8:1). Colossians 1:14 tells us that through God's beloved Son, "we have received redemption, the forgiveness of offenses." The Amplified Bible translates the last phrase this way: "the forgiveness of our sins (and the cancellation of sins' penalty)." God's gracious forgiveness of our offense is to be the measure of our gracious forgiveness of others (Ephesians 4:32).

To some people, forgiveness could seem like weakness or letting an undeserving person win, but it's not connected to weakness or even to emotions. Instead, forgiveness is an act of will. Forgiveness isn't granted because an individual deserves to be forgiven. Nobody deserves to be forgiven. Forgiveness must be a deliberate act of affection, mercy, and grace. Forgiveness must be a decision to not hold something against another person despite what he or she has done to you.

As believers, our relationship with God is reestablished, but what about our relationship with our fellow individuals? The Bible states that when someone offends us, we are under an obligation to God to forgive that person. Jesus is extremely clear on this point in Matthew 6:14–15 when he said, "For if you forgive people once they sin against you, your heavenly Father also will forgive you. But if you don't forgive others their wrongs, your Father won't forgive your wrongs."

Refusing to forgive is wrong. If we receive forgiveness from God, we then have to provide it to others who have wronged us. We cannot hold grudges or go for revenge. We must trust God for justice and then forgive the one that offended us. That doesn't mean we must forget the offense, however; usually, that's beyond our power. Forgiveness means releasing the opposite from blame, leaving the matter in God's care, and then move on.

We may resume a relationship with the individual if we had one, or we might not if one didn't exist before. Certainly, the victim of a criminal offense has no obligation to become a close acquaintance with the criminal. We hand it over to the courts and to God to judge them.

Nothing compares to the liberty we feel once we learn to forgive others. Once we choose not to forgive, we become captives to bitterness. We are the ones most devastated by holding on to forgiveness.

In his book *Forgive and Forget*, Lewis Smedes wrote these profound words about forgiveness: "When you release the incorrect doer from the wrong, you narrow a malignant neoplasm out of your inner life. You set a prisoner free, but you discover that the real prisoner was yourself."

Forgiveness must be a choice. Many of us still think that forgiveness is an emotion you either feel or you don't feel. But that's not what's at the guts of forgiveness. At its heart, forgiveness is an act of the desire, a choice.

Forgiveness is selecting to not hold an offense against someone. It is choosing not to linger over the offense or continue to rehearse it in your mind.

Forgiveness is deciding not to keep a record (or keep score).

The scripture tells us in 1 Corinthians 13:5 that love isn't rude. It's not self-seeking. It's not easily angered. It keeps no record of wrongs.

The ability to forgive and to let go of past offense is certainly a critical tool in marriage. Additionally, having the ability to forgive may be a tool to keep yourself healthy both emotionally and physically.

In fact, forgiving and letting go could also be one among the foremost important ways to keep you and your marriage going strong. Some transgressions are so harmful that a civil partnership can't survive, but forgiveness can still play a part.

If you hold onto old offenses, disappointments, petty annoyances, betrayals, insensitivity, and anger, you're wasting both your time and your energy. Nursing your heartbreak (whether real or perceived) for too long can eventually make it become more hurtful and produce extreme bitterness.

Lack of forgiveness also can wear you down. Being unforgiving takes both a physical and emotional toll. Resentment gains speed and chips away at the expense of your well-being and your relationship. Instead, share your feelings with your spouse.

Health experts at Johns Hopkins convey a massage that the act of forgiveness can reduce the danger of attack, lower cholesterol levels, improve sleep, reduce pain, lower your vital signs, and reduce levels of hysteria, depression, and stress. Research have also suggested that forgiveness provides substantial benefits.

## How to Forgive Your Partner

Forgetting those things behind and reaching for those things ahead

Philippians 3:13

There are different techniques you'll use to seek out an area of forgiveness once you have experienced betrayal. Consider each method and find the mixture that works best for you.

The hurt you've suffered may make a difference. Certainly, it's harder to forgive a spouse for years of infidelity than it is for a minor mistake like forgetting to pay a bill on time.

First, you must be open and receive forgiveness at all times.

Make a deliberate decision to forgive your spouse.

Think of a relaxing place or do something to distract yourself from dwelling on those thoughts when images of the betrayal or hurt flash in your mind.

Refrain from throwing a mistake back in your spouse's face at a later date; don't use it as ammunition in an argument.

Accept that you simply may never know the rationale for the transgression, behavior, or mistake.

Refrain from seeking revenge or retribution; the urge to get even will only extend the pain, and there is the possibility that this would probably not cause you to feel better anyway.

Remember that forgiveness doesn't mean that you simply condone hurtful behavior.

Be patient with yourself. Having the ability to forgive your spouse takes time. Don't attempt to hurry the method.

Seek professional guidance to assist you in abandoning and forgiving if you're still unable to let go. Otherwise, you end up dwelling on the betrayal or hurt.

It is also very important to know how to seek forgiveness when you happen to be the offender.

If you're the partner who has caused hurt, you'll invite forgiveness in an attempt to rebuild trust within the relationship.

Remember to offer yourself and your partner time when working through the method. Here are some tips you may consider:

- Show genuine contrition and remorse for the pain that you've caused.
- Be willing to form a commitment to not hurt your partner again by repeating the hurtful behavior.
- Accept the results of the action that created the hurt.
- Be hospitable in making amends.
- Make a heartfelt and spoken apology; this includes an idea of action to make things right.
- Be patient together with your partner. Having the ability to forgive regularly, takes time. Don't dismiss your spouse's feelings of betrayal by telling them to "get over it."

Marriage, like other intimate relationships, needs forgiveness to thrive. Remember that everybody makes mistakes. We all have bad or grumpy days. Most people say things they do not mean every now and then. Everyone must forgive and be forgiven.

This is easier if the one that hurt you is attempting to form amends and seek forgiveness; it's harder if your partner isn't remorseful. But even then, you'll find value in offering forgiveness.

No healthy relationship, especially a marriage, is often sustained over an extended period of time without forgiveness. But remember that forgiveness isn't absolution.

Forgiveness may be a conscious decision and a skill of releasing feelings of resentment. Letting go can provide you and your partner with the tools to process and advance.

# Communication: The Game Changer

Communication in Marriage

Open channels to express clear and meaningful conversation together

If someone asks you what the true basis of a cheerful married life is, you'll say love, commitment, honesty, and other such things. However, how often can we mention the importance of communication during a marriage? Simply because two people are spending most of their time under one roof doesn't mean that they convey effectively with one another. To sustain a cheerful marriage and have a robust bond together with your spouse, there must be effective communication between both partners. Communication isn't only words; it's about actions or non-verbal communication that holds great significance too. Let me acquaint you with the importance of communication, tips to enhance it, and various other aspects associated with it.

Realize that communication in marriage plays a way more vital role than we will fathom. It's important to open channels to possess clear and meaningful communication together with your spouse for there to be trust and understanding, which suggests a far better relationship together with your spouse.

## Importance of Communication during a Marriage

Why is communication so important to possess for an extended, fulfilling relationship together with your better half? What's the role of communication in marriage? Well, here are some points that emphasize the importance of communication in marriage:

1. **No communication implies no interest.**

    If you do not know what's happening in your partner's life or what issues they'll be handling, you'll not be ready to understand or empathize. This can slowly cause a scarcity of interest in each other's lives and thus strain relationships; therefore, it's important to possess a good communication skill.

2. **Better understanding**

    Couples who often talk, discuss their lives together, or communicate with one another regularly not only have a far better understanding with one another, but it also helps them to possess a stronger bond with one another. Once you understand your spouse and therefore the situations they'll be handling, there would be less misunderstanding or ambiguity.

3. **Better marital satisfaction**

If you've opened the doors of effective communication together with your spouse, you're more likely to experience a cheerful and peaceful relationship. Better communication means better satisfaction during a relationship in which you discuss everything with one another and thus resulting in lesser fights or quarrels.

4. **Better trust, honesty, and respect**

Marriage must be a two-way thing; you can't just keep expecting everything without giving. Therefore, if you're honest together with your spouse, and you provide and receive comforts or share other issues with complete honesty, it helps in building better trust during a relationship.

5. **Better connection**

Communication is a way of expressing your feelings and emotions toward your spouse. We understand that it's not important to be precise in the word of love and affection that you simply have for your spouse. However, being expressive and vocal is one of the simplest ways of exhibiting your emotions toward your spouse, which might cause a far better connection.

However, during communication, there are some mistakes that couples make that can lead to misunderstanding. Let us briefly highlight these common mistakes couples make in marriage and the way to unravel them.

Here are some common mistakes that majority of the people usually make and the way we will solve them effectively:

1. **More "me" in marriage**

When you get married, the connection is for you both. However, at times we may forget that, and marriage becomes more about you than about your spouse. For instance, on your anniversary you would like your spouse to make *you* feel special and take *you* out to dinner; or *you* want to travel to a specific destination, and if for some reason that doesn't happen, *you* will not go and etc. All of these show that your happiness or consent is more important than your partner's.

How to resolve it: You must consider your partner's interests too. This can be possible once you communicate better with one another. Ask your partner and know what they desire or don't desire or what their idea of celebration or other things of such is.

2. **Shouting at the spouse**

Every relationship has its challenges, and these are sure to happen. However, if your spouse makes an error regardless of how trivial or grave it is, it's not okay to shout or say nasty things to your spouse. It's imperative to know that everybody makes mistakes, and once you shout or scold your spouse, you say hurtful things. Words uttered during anger often scar the opposite person's feelings or emotions, and it is often more evident when there's less or zero communication in a marriage.

How to resolve it: Even if you've got a legitimate point to be angry, don't be. Ensure you subtly convey your point without creating any ill feelings or negativity. The simplest way is, you wait until you let your anger pass and then ask your spouse about it. The purpose isn't to point out displeasure or disappointment, but it's about not committing an equivalent mistake again.

### 3.  Don't compare or compete with each other

One of the silliest mistakes that wedded couples can make is comparing or competing with their spouse. This error could also be more pronounced or evident in people with similar professional backgrounds or jobs. You'll gloat about your professional achievements or accomplishments together with your spouse or mention their failures or setbacks negatively. Well, it's acceptable to possess a competitive spirit or healthy competition with one another, but at no point do you have to demean your spouse. Lack of communication in marriage can worsen things.

How to resolve it: The number one thing to understand is that even if you're doing separate jobs, you both are one entity or bonded amorously—this suggests that your relationship is supreme than anything. Be encouraging if your spouse defaults and be proud when your spouse excels. There's no room for any comparison or competition between two people that love one another.

Communication is certainly a great tool to keep marriage going. There are different types of good communication that can strengthen your marriage. Let us consider these types of communication.

You may have different sorts of communication together with your spouse and strengthen the bond of your marriage. If you would like to understand the types of communication that strengthen a relationship effectively or the way to open communication during a marriage, well, here are some ways you'll do that:

1. **Informal communication**

    You talk about everything that matters or other silly things that happened during the day. You laugh together and have an excellent time talking about some lighthearted aspects of life. This type of communication helps in building a stronger bond together with your spouse because you share fun and happy moments.

2. **Mention the challenges**

    Every marriage has lows and highs, and it's important to debate and evaluate the strengths and weaknesses of your marriage with one another. Such conversations help the connection to grow, and they also assist in making any important changes or decisions in life.

    When our spouse has offended or disappointed us, as an example, or we disagreed on something critical or we have conversations that provoked deep grief, anger, or confusion when we've lost employment or we're handling illness, these are challenges that we must learn to handle with grace and understanding.

Conversations attached to challenges can help us to develop both as individuals and as a couple. They will expose our blind spots or lead us to form important and necessary changes in our lives.

Although this is a critical conversation to possess during a marriage relationship, it is delicate, too, so we must make good effort to interact in a gracious manner. This also requires the use of our greatest active-listening skills ("So I hear you saying..."). Validate whatever emotions that are expressed and be willing to supply forgiveness if it's needed.

**3. Life-giving communication**

This is a proactive conversation that's not instigated directly to some need or demand, unlike the communications mentioned above. These sorts of communications emphasize having insightful discussions that include talking about your fears, desires, dreams, hopes, etc. This includes meaningful conversations which will cause meaningful relationships. These are very intimate conversations because it gives you glimpses of your spouse's inner life.

Now, the two sorts of communication I outlined above are, for the foremost part, natural conversation skills for a husband and wife to possess. We engage in chitchat because it is fun and that we want to share. But if all our conversations revolved around chitchat, administration, and conflict resolution, we'd get disinterested in lecturing one another. Some couples seem to only run out of things to speak about, and it causes me to wonder if they ignored the third critical sort of communication, which is the life-giving conversation.

The two modes of communication above are reactive conversations—spurred on by some need or event. This third mode of communication is usually overlooked because it's proactive. Life-giving conversations are about getting to know your partner better and strengthening the bonds between you. They're playful and affirming. They express gratitude and demonstrate curiosity. Ask the spouse questions you've never asked before. Unpack hopes and dreams.

The first two sorts of conversations will monopolize some time unless you intentionally make space for this one. But how?

Let's talk about a thought provoked by Dr. Terri Orbuch. Studying nearly four hundred couples over thirty years, Orbuch discovered that happy couples spend at least ten minutes every day talking about meaningful things.

It's easy to ascertain why these important talks can make a relationship very meaningful. They mean a commitment to understanding your partner's inner life—his or her hopes and fears, needs, desires, and dreams. They show your partner that he or she is the most vital person in your life whom you would like to understand everything there's to understand. These are great conversations. They're statements of intimate commitment.

So agree with your spouse to spend a minimum of ten minutes a day talking about anything aside from work, the household, kids, problems, or maybe your relationship. Specialize in the subjects that matter deep down—the subjects that expand your understanding of your mate.

Take joy in rediscovering your spouse over and over. A whole life together isn't enough to really know your husband or wife because they're always changing. That's the sweetness of marriage!

In acquiring the best communication skills, there are dos and don'ts. If you desire to get the best out of your marriage, you must be deliberate about your conversations—the things to say and the things not to say.

## Dos and Don'ts to Enhance Your Communication in Marriage

We will now discuss some marriage communication tips or some dos and don'ts that you simply want to practice to enhance your communication in marriage.

1. **Try to be specific.**

   Whenever you would like to make a point, make sure you're specific about it. Don't beat around the bush or mention random and insignificant things. Avoid generalizing by making statements like "You always say/do this." This might not solve the purpose; instead, you'll find yourself hurting your spouse.

2. **Be respectful.**

   No matter what kind of conversation you and your spouse are having, it's important to be respectful toward it. By being an honest listener, you show that you simply respect your partner. Once you listen, your partner will do an equivalent once you need to say something.

**3.  Don't nag or taunt.**

No one likes getting picked on or shouted at, and therefore the same holds for your spouse. You can't keep making your partner feel guilty or liable for his past mistakes whenever you would make a point. Your partner wants to feel loved and cared for, and each time you taunt your partner, it not only causes hurt and pain, but it also affects your relationship. Also, never involve relations or friends once you have arguments.

**4.  Don't jump to conclusions.**

Do not assume things or make your own stories without having a word together with your spouse. You'll get angry that your spouse didn't pick up your call without even understanding or giving them an opportunity to explain why it happened. Ask your spouse about what's bothering you regarding them and know the reality behind their side of the story.

**5.  Make your conversations regular.**

No matter how busy you are or what type of work you've got, confirm that you're taking out time every day to have some meaningful conversations together with your spouse. If you can't consider anything to speak about, get goofy or silly and share some hearty laughs. It's vital to talk with your spouse regularly to keep the love flowing within the relationship.

6. **No blame games.**

Even if you're mad because your spouse did something wrong, it's not recommended to start out playing the blame game. Possibly your spouse may have had self-realization that an error was committed, and necessary measures may be taken to make amendments. However, if there are not any realizations, it's always better to make your points subtly and politely instead of hitting the opposite person with all the blames.

7. **Don't believe in online chatting.**

When you are away at work or far away from home, chatting through a medium of online chatting is convenient to an extent, but it cannot substitute meaningful one-to-one conversations or phone conversations. Sometimes online modes of communication can cause misunderstandings and confusions and may strain happy relationships.

8. **Don't be defensive.**

If your partner must bring out some complaints or issues against you, it's important to concentrate on them intently without being defensive about it. It's equally hard for your partner to bring his or her flaws ahead of you.

Make sure you listen and take effective measures to unravel the difficulty instead of getting all defensive about the entire issue.

9. **Be tolerant.**

We all have different preferences, likes, or dislikes, and therefore the same goes for two people that are married to each other. You'll like watching football, but your spouse loves tennis. Be appreciative and tolerant of each other's hobbies, choices, and other such aspects rather than complaining about them. Once you become receptive, your partner will too.

10. **Express positive feelings.**

Most folks may mention our worries, tensions, fears, and other such negative feelings instead of mentioning positive feelings like love, compassion, humility, and etc. Make sure you include more positive talks, which might include complimenting one another, showing love and care, and other such positive feelings.

## Reasons to Speak

There are very important but overlooked reasons why you must speak out in a proper manner in marriage. It is therefore very vital for you not to assume that your spouse knows or understands. You must verbalize your thoughts and concerns for a proper understanding. When you learn to speak out properly, you will realize some critical benefits that many people tend to ignore. Let me briefly highlight some of these benefits.

*It saves you money*

There's little question about it; poor communications are often costly. Flowers, candy, and gifts large and small are regularly offered by a spouse who said the "wrong thing" or did not say the "right thing." Once you check out costly mistakes in marriage, the bulk of them are a result of poor communications.

*Yeah*, *sure*, and *whatever* could seem like an efficient way of handling your husband or wife once they want to speak, but it's not. Sooner or later, an unresolved issue has to be discussed. Therefore, taking the time to listen to your spouse when he or she wants to speak with you will ultimately be a time saver. You won't need to return to the start and begin again because you communicated clearly and honestly at the right time.

### It earns points for the longer term

Whenever you and your spouse have a satisfying conversation, you build credit toward future communication. Both of you recognize and expect that you simply are going to be ready to share because you've got a record of success.

### It's important for your health

Good communication in marriage reduces or lowers stress for two reasons. First, it allows you to settle the strain between you; and second, it allows you to "vent" a number of your anxieties from other areas of your life. Couples report that their partner is that person they can fully trust. "I can tell him anything" and "I know he will listen and understand how I feel" should be the report.

### It allows you to consider other important things

Have you, at some point, found yourself continuing a discussion you previously had while you were at work? *I should have said this*, you tell yourself. "Oh, it is true? Well, what about the time you did…" Perhaps you're so upset about an unfinished conversation earlier within the day that you simply call your spouse to either apologize or get another point across. Listening and talking effectively resolves the difficulty and frees your mind to consider other tasks.

## It builds up your relationship

Couples who don't communicate are in peril of losing love and affection for each other. All relationships are nourished by effective communications. If you don't talk with your parents, siblings, coworkers, children, or your partner, you lose touch with them, and your relationship withers.

## It helps you learn more about yourself

Have you ever tried to elucidate your thoughts or feelings to somebody else and, through the conversation, you finish up in a different place from where you started? Putting your thoughts into words compels you to clarify them. Talking and listening also allow you to fine-tune your ideas.

## Less hassle

"Why won't you ask me?" "I know something is troubling you. What is it?" "Don't just walk away. Ask me. Please!"

Be honest. Avoiding communications is more costly than communicating. So why not just talk? Or does one like being pursued? Does being silent offer you more control over the situation? While it's going to seem that way, ultimately, you'll have a spouse who will trust you less. Giving your partner the gift of some time to speak things through will make your life simpler at the end of the day.

## *You would possibly learn something new*

The person you're married to isn't the person you initially met. Neither are you an equivalent. Every day brings entirely new experiences, thoughts, dreams, and plans. It's a guarantee that if you're good at communicating, you'll discover new things about one another.

These discoveries identify two directions from where you are now. You'll discover experiences from your spouse's childhood that you simply never knew. You don't know them because the person you've come to love has them concealed in their memory. They do not remember until some new experience triggers a remembrance.

You see a toddler run into the road and your husband says, "I almost got hit by a car when I was that age." What follows may be a story of childhood excitement, parental fear, and lessons learned that come pouring out from the distant past. It'd explain why he drives so slowly in areas with children or offer you insight into how he will react when your child does something similar a year from now.

It is, however, so vital for you to know the right words to use when communicating with your spouse. Right choice of words is very important as it facilitates affection. At every point of communication, you must endeavor to choose your words carefully to avoid some costly mistakes in communication. Listed below are some of the kind words you can use to facilitate good communication in your marriage.

## Kind Words to Say

- You make me smile.
- I think of you.
- You've got great ideas.
- You're hardworking.
- You make a difference.
- How can I assist you?
- I'm sorry.
- Will you forgive me?
- I forgive you.
- You're loved.
- You're creative.
- Great discovery.
- I like you.
- You're kind.
- I prefer working with you.
- I love the way you do things.
- You're brave.
- We will learn from mistakes.
- Mistakes help us grow.
- Continue the great work.
- I prefer you.
- Thanks for being you.
- God made you special.
- You've got tons to supply.
- You're right.
- You're fun to be with.
- What an incredible idea.
- What else do I want except you?
- Let's roll in the hay together.
- Good thinking.
- That was a great thing to do.

- You've got special gifts and skills.
- You're always available.
- Let's pray about it together.
- You're good at the things you do.
- You've got an enormous heart.
- You've got the simplest smile.
- Great discovery.
- You're kind.
- You're fun to be with.
- Your heart is so kind.
- You're an honest friend.
- You're an honest listener.
- You're important to me.
- You figured it out.
- Well done.
- Many thanks for helping me.
- I would like to listen to what you've got to say.
- Many thanks for following directions.
- That's wonderful news.
- Your ideas matter.
- Many thanks for sharing.
- Tell me more.
- I trust you.
- I'm pleased with you.
- I appreciate you.
- You mean the whole world to me.
- You belong.
- I appreciate your attention.
- Thanks for telling me the truth.
- Thanks for trusting me.
- We'd like your help.
- You're joyful.
- You're beautiful inside and out.

- I'm here for you.
- I prefer spending time with you.
- You're helpful.
- You made my day.
- You are such a great person.
- You have done well.

Words that express kindness and gentleness toward another person express the goodness in you. Your spouse deserves to hear that you care and are paying attention. Of course, we don't give to receive; however, to get something back unexpectedly becomes a bonus in marriage.

## How to Have a Meaningful Conversation

Set a day and time to discuss only one topic.

Check with your spouse if the day and time is good for him/her.

Advise your spouse of the topic. Be courteous enough to allow them to gather their thoughts and ideas of the topic.

Be on time. Any preparation needed with finishing up work, getting the children situated, mealtime, etc. should all be complete and out of the way.

If the conversation goes over your allotted time or negative issues of the past show up or the topic changes, it's time to dismiss the discussion and reschedule.

The intent for meaningful conversation is to always come away with a resolution to the conflict.

# Compromise: The Equalizer

Compromise in marriage is so vital as it brings both parties to a middle point of agreement.

The definition of a compromise is when two sides give up some personal demands to meet somewhere in the middle that is beneficial to both parties.

It is an agreement in an argument in which the people involved reduce their demands or change their opinions to agree.

Fights happen. They're part of life. But these small fights and spats sometimes compile and form into bomb cyclones of quarrels where curses fly. Assuming that a husband knows the line he crossed when he used such language and wants to bridge the gap between himself and his partner, the first thing that needs to happen is to take a break.

"The vital thing to remember, after an argument gets to that level of heatedness, is the concept of repair," Ball said. "You need to get the relationship back to normal as quickly as possible."

For many couples, this means putting more effort to settle down. It is referred to as "physiological self-soothing." That means just walking away, taking a deep breath, and waiting till your heart rate calms down to a normal state. This kind of break can take ten minutes. It could take the whole night. It could even take one day or two. But the most vital part of this practice is when both partners come back to the conversation.

Now, when the conversation takes place, the person who is the offender needs to come out clean. But they do not want to explain why they said it. It is oftentimes not easy to say "I'm sorry I did this. Here's the reason why I did it." When you are trying to reconnect and repair, do not justify your act. Apologize and let it be.

This can be difficult. Even if they feel as if they were within their right to say what they said, there should be no effort to justify the act—a sign of defensiveness.

The truth is everyone says things in an argument that they later wish they didn't. Saying that they did not mean to say those words doesn't dull their impact.

It's important to take ownership for the things you said out of anger. Don't focus on what your partner said as that will deflect from the responsibility for your actions.

Typically, when one partner can do this, the other is more willing to follow suit by owning their part of the argument.

Compromise is an important aspect of any successful marriage. For two individuals to work together as a team, each individual has to give and take at some points in time. But truthfully, many of us do not have the idea how to truly compromise.

Unless we become well skilled in the art of compromise, our relationship can quickly go down into feelings of dissatisfaction and strife. Not to mention a depriving sense of being all alone in the relationship. Most people are good at making decisions for themselves, but once you commit to a relationship, you have to consider the needs, wants, and happiness of your partner. That holds even more so when you reside together and get wedded. It takes effort, but this step-by-step guide will help you learn how to compromise in a marriage.

## Ways to Compromise in Marriage

As we look into these steps, realize that compromise is not giving up what is godly and embracing what is ungodly. These are, however, steps that will help you to properly discern and conform to the vision and the purpose of God concerning your marriage. It means to selflessly give up your selfish demands and then conform or embrace godly counsel and demands that benefit both parties and ensure the success of the marriage.

## *Communicate your needs clearly*

Use *I* statements to communicate to your partner exactly what you need or desire in the relationship. You may say, "I want to reside in the city because it's very near to my work, which will reduce my commute. I also enjoy the excitement of it, and I'm bored here in the countryside." Or you could say, "I think I am ready to have kids now because we're married, financially balanced, and my biological clock is ticking fast." It's important to speak up for yourself without making assumptions concerning your spouse's needs or wants and also to express what you want and why. This will enhance the understanding of your reasons and aid the consideration of your spouse.

## *Listen (without interrupting)*

After you have expressed your wants and offered an explanation as to why something is vital to you, give your spouse an opportunity to respond. Allow them to talk and don't interject. Pay special attention to the things they're saying and try not to reject their thoughts instantly.

"Disagreements are best resolved when each individual's needs are assumed to be legitimate and important," Seltzer said.

If your partner responds with a detailed contradiction, then you should repeat what you heard without an evil desire to make sure you're on the same page. You could put it this way and say, "So you're saying that you prefer to live in the suburbs because your workplace is around here, and the city is too noisy and chaotic for your liking?" You want to let your spouse know that you esteem and value their needs and desires too.

## *Carefully weigh your options*

Consider all your options and recall that there are more than two options for every matter. You could reside in the city, you could live in the country sides, or you could live in a suburb closer to the city that has high-rise apartments and enough public transportation to allow you to have the best of both worlds. Before concluding, you could look at your budget and the cost of living in both the city and country-side. Remember to think about the choice as though you are part of a pair and not just for yourself. You must give zero tolerance for selfishness in this matter.

## *Put yourself in your partner's shoes*

Truly, understanding your spouse can be difficult, especially when your desires cloud your judgment. That's why you need to step out of your mind for some time and consider your spouse's point of view and feelings. How would they be affected if they go on to agree to your own opinion? What would be the positive and negative effects for them? What do you think about their different points of view? What sort of sacrifices would they be making in the event that they gave up to agree with your ideas? Let your spouse understand what responses you come up with to these questions and offer empathy.

## *Consider what is fair*

For compromise in a marriage to work out well, one person shouldn't always be the doormat. That is to say you can't always get your way, and your spouse can't (and most likely will not) always give in to you and agree to your needs.

Also, you have to put to consideration the fairness of each choice. If you move to the city, you may have an easier workplace and be more delighted in the speedy lifestyle. But will your spouse's commute double? Will they be put out by the fast life? Is that fair to them?

## Make a decision and stick to it

After you've considered your options and considered your spouse's feelings and the fairness of the situation, it's important to make a decision together and hold on to it. If you've been completely honest while performing all the other steps, you should come to a resolution that you both approve of and that won't leave you with any doubts.

## Check in with one another

When there's give-and-take in a marriage union, one or both of you are liable to make a sacrifice or giving up certain things you wanted or needed. If this occurs often, you or your spouse may start to feel taken for granted or ignored. This can result in resentment to build, which can break down a marriage. Check in with one another to make sure there are no anger or hurt feelings. Make sure that when you agree to a compromise that you will not still hold the sacrifice over your spouse's head, doubt your decision, or be upset about it. You have to make the choice, stick with it, and move forward positively.

## Compassion Starts at Home

I believe that it is our innate nature to be compassionate toward our fellow men and women, but we sometimes lose sight of this when it comes to our closest companions—our spouse, especially if we've been married for many years.

You may not want to admit it, but we often practice learned behaviors that we reap benefits from, such as complaining about every little pain or ache to get more attention. This usually happens when we're feeling neglected and we haven't communicated this truth to our mates. Okay, let me back up. Maybe it's just me, but I doubt it.

I know in my own experience that I have done this before, and I've witnessed my husband doing it. Thank goodness for the Holy Spirit that quickens our spirit to let us know when there's misalignment in how we treat each other in marriage and even in other relationships.

Here's my story of how God reminded me that compassion starts at home.

I have been a business owner for well over a decade. During the early years of building my business, I was blessed in that my husband was retired and he was very supportive.

I was still working a full-time, stressful career putting in twelve to fourteen-hour days and then coming home to work on the business four to six hours a night. My husband took over all my household duties: cooking, cleaning, laundry, and grocery shopping. All I had to do was come home, eat, and work on my business. Talk about being blessed.

Well over the years, I know that this took a toll on our marriage. I had thrown myself so heavily into growing my business that I forgot to grow my marriage. One day, my husband told me that he missed his wife. I knew then it was time for a change.

You know how we are made aware of things but then fail to truly act on them until it becomes necessary? That was my story. Sure, I cut back on working too many hours building the business. I started to enjoy dinners with my husband, we implemented a date night again, and we started to really enjoy each other's company again. But my mind was still on business and all the things I had to do to keep striving for success.

Then, my husband was hit with a terrible bout of the shingles. It was bad. It showed up in his face. The pain he endured was almost unbearable for him. He would scream every time the sharp pain that attacked his facial nerves would strike. We spent many nights sitting up because he couldn't sleep. I would just hold his hand and tell him to squeeze my hand when the pain hit.

In the midst of this, I had thoughts of, *It's not that bad. He's just trying to get attention.* Well, the Holy Spirit reminded me that I wasn't being compassionate toward him and his current situation. To be honest, I would almost shut down in my mind thinking that if I gave him too much attention, he would just continue to complain about the pain and not *man up*. How selfish of me.

His struggles with shingles continued for about three months, hot and heavy. This time frame ran up against a very important event I had scheduled to attend, and my husband has planned to join me. This event is an annual event that I attend to support my largest client. It's an all-expenses paid event for me, and I get paid to be there for my client. The event is a five-day event.

My husband, being the supportive man that he is, would never ask me to miss an important event and lose money. Being true to his character, he said, "You go on. I'll be okay."

Here, I was faced with a major decision: attend the event and make money or stay home with my husband who was really struggling. I'll admit, I thought about losing thousands of dollars and missing out on a great time hanging out with my clients. But then, I was once again reminded that compassion starts at home.

Deep in my heart, I knew the right thing to do would be to stay home with my husband and support him during this trying time. But being a purpose-driven entrepreneur, I wanted to show up and support my clients. My heart was screaming, *Compassion starts at home.*

So I followed my heart and the guidance of the Holy Spirit and made the decision to stay home with my husband. I know this decision was the beginning of a whole new perspective and way of being in my marriage. This was the decision that led to me being more mindful of my husband's needs and structuring my business to align with what's most important—our marriage.

After this series of events, I made the decision to restructure my business so that I only work four days a week. I now spend my Fridays and the weekend nurturing and loving my husband. I realized that he is the most important person in my life, and I could not be the successful businesswoman that I am today without his support. I also realized that if I didn't show compassion at home, how could I authentically share compassion with my clients and others?

My strongest advice, keep compassion for each other alive in your marriage. Nurture each other and your relationship to always be mindful of what you both need.

Having a business you truly enjoy is rewarding, but having peace at home is even more rewarding.

V. Priester

# Listening Skills

Listening skills is the ability to concentrate and effectively interpret what people are saying. It is the power to accurately receive and interpret messages within the communication process.

Listening is important to all or to any effective communication. Without the power to concentrate effectively, messages are easily misunderstood. As a result, communication breaks down and therefore the sender of the message can easily become frustrated or irritated.

If there's one communication skill you ought to aim to master, then listening is it. Studies have shown that, whereas speaking raises vital sign, attentive listening can bring it down.

Let me also point out to us here that listening isn't an equivalent to hearing.

Hearing implies the sounds that enter your ears. It's a physical process that as long as you do not have any hearing problems, it occurs automatically.

Listening, nevertheless, requires more than that. It requires focus and concentrated effort, both mental and sometimes physical also.

Listening implies listening not only to the story but to how it's told, the utilization of language and voice, and the way the other person uses his or her body. In other words, it means being conscious of both verbal and nonverbal messages. Your ability to perceive and understand these messages depends on the degree to which you concentrate effectively during the listening process.

Listening isn't a passive process. The listener can be actively engaged within the process as the speaker. The phrase *active listening* is employed to explain this process of being fully involved. There must be a purpose behind every communication, and the aim of listening is to discern that purpose. Let me quickly highlight some of them for a better understanding.

## The Purpose of Listening

There is little question concerning effective listening as an important life skill. Why is listening so important?

Listening serves several possible purposes, and therefore, the purpose of listening will depend upon things and the nature of the communication. Here are the possible purposes:

- To specifically understand the messages being communicated, you must remove distractions and preconceptions in order to gain the full understanding of the message being communicated
- To gain a full and accurate comprehension of the speaker's point of view and notion
- To critically consider what is being said
- To observe the non-verbal signals following what's being said to reinforce comprehension
- To show interest, concern, and focus
- To help the speaker to speak fully, openly, and sincerely
- To bring up a selflessness approach, putting the speaker first
- To come to a shared and agreed comprehension and acceptance of both sides' views

Nevertheless, there are certain hindrances or barriers to effective listening. These barriers will hinder the real aim or goal of effective listening. Let us quickly consider these barriers and offer a way out.

## Barriers to Effective Listening

Most times, our main concern while listening is to formulate ways to reply. This is often not a function of listening. We should always attempt to focus fully on what's being said and the way it's being said to fully understand the speaker more.

To improve the method of effective listening, it is often helpful to have a good understanding of these barriers to effective listening, or put differently, ineffective listening.

For example, one common problem is that rather than listening closely to what someone is saying, we frequently get distracted after a sentence or two and instead start to believe what we are getting to say back or believe unrelated things. This suggests that we don't fully hear the remainder of the speaker's message. Concentrating on just a fragment of what is being said will deprive you of the full understanding of the purpose of the communication.

This issue is attributed, in part, to the distinction between average rate of speech and average rate of processing. Average rates of speech are between 125 and 175 words a minute, whereas we will process on the average between 400 and 800 words a minute. It's a standard habit for the listener to use their spare time while they are allowing their thoughts to daydream or believe other things instead of focusing on what is actually being said. Of course, it is clear that what the speaker is talking about can also affect how well we listen. Generally, we discover that it is easier to focus if the speaker is fluent in their speech, features a familiar accent, and speaks at an appropriate loudness. It's harder, for instance, to pay attention to somebody who is speaking without a specified time and who is really not audible, especially if they're conveying complex information.

We can also get distracted by the speaker's appearance or by what somebody else is saying, which sounds more interesting.

These issues not only affect you, but you're likely to point out your lack of attention in your visual communication.

It's important to not jump to conclusions about what you see and listen to. You ought to always seek clarification to make sure that your understanding is correct.

## Steps to Effective Listening

In today's high-tech, high-speed, high-stress world, interaction is more important than ever, yet we seem to devote less and fewer time to pay attention to one another. Genuine listening has turned to a rare gift—the gift of your time. It helps build relationships, solve issues, ensure understanding, settle conflicts, and aids accuracy. At work, effective listening implies fewer errors and fewer time wastage. At home, it helps build up resourceful, self-reliant kids who can solve their problems. Listening builds friendships and careers. It saves money and marriages. There is need for us to deliberately build this skill as it is vital to the sustenance of homes. Let me quickly highlight some tips that will help you develop effective listening skills.

Here are tips to help you build effective listening ability.

**Step 1: Look at the face of the speaker and keep eye contact.**
Talking to a person while they scan the space, study a display screen, or gaze out the window is like trying to hit a moving target. What proportion of the person's divided attention are you getting? Fifty percent? Five percent? If the person happens to be your child, you would possibly

demand, "Look at me when I'm talking to you." But that's not the kind of thing we are saying to a devotee, friend, or coworker.

In most Western traditions, eye contact is taken into account as a basic ingredient of effective communication. Once we talk, we glance at one another in the eyes. That does not imply that you just cannot keep up with a conversation from across the room; but if the conversation continues for any length of your time, you (or the opposite person) will rise and move. The need for better communication will draw you closer.

Give your conversational partners the gesture of turning to face them. Let go of papers, books, the phone, and other distractions. Shyness, uncertainty, shame, guilt, or other emotions, alongside cultural taboos, can inhibit eye contact in some people under some circumstances. Excuse the opposite guy but stay focused on yourself.

**Step 2: Be attentive but relaxed.**

Now that you've truly made eye contact, relax. You do not need to stare fixedly at the opposite person. You'll look now and then and keep it up. The important thing is to pay attention. The dictionary says that *to attend* to another person is to be present, to offer attention, apply or direct yourself, pay attention, and remain able to serve.

Mentally avoid distractions like background activity and noise. Also, try not to focus on the speaker's accent or speech mannerisms to the point where they become distractions. Finally, do not be distracted by your thoughts, emotions, or biases.

**Step 3: Keep your mind open.**

Listen without having to judge the other person or without mentally criticizing the thing she says to you. If what she says disturbs you, make every effort to stay focused and not let it linger. But don't tell yourself, "Well, that was a stupid move." As soon as you enjoy being judgmental, you've given up your effectiveness as a good listener.

Listen without jumping to conclusions. Recall that the speaker is using language to represent the thoughts and feelings inside her brain. You do not know what those thoughts and feelings are and therefore the only way you will find out is by listening.

Don't be a sentence-grabber. Occasionally you will realize that your partner can't slow his mental pace enough to concentrate effectively, so he tries to hurry up yours by interrupting and finishing your sentences. This can cause a person to lose focus on the meaning of what's being said. After a few times of this, it is usually normal to ask, "Can you even listen to what I have to say?" Understanding is a very important part of listening skills.

**Step 4: Hear the words and determine what the speaker is saying.**

Allow your mind to make a mental model of the knowledge being communicated. Whether a literal picture or an appointment of abstract concepts, your brain will do the required work if you stay focused, with your senses fully alert. When listening for long stretches, consider and remember keywords and phrases.

When you are being addressed, listen. Don't spend the time planning what to say next. You cannot rehearse and be attentive at the same time. Think only about what the opposite person is saying.

Finally, consider what's being said even if it bores you. If your thoughts start to wander, instantly force yourself to refocus.

## Step 5: Don't interrupt, and do not impose your "solutions."

It is important not to interrupt during conversation. Interruption cuts the flow of understanding. Interrupting sends a range of messages. It says:

"I'm more important than you are."

"What I have to say is more interesting, accurate, or relevant."

"I don't care what you think."

"I do not have time for your opinion."

"This isn't a conversation. It is a contest, and I am going to win."

We all think and talk at different rates. If you're a fast thinker and an agile talker, the burden is on you to relax your pace for the slower, more thoughtful communicator—or for the guy who has trouble expressing himself.

When taking note, refrain from suggesting solutions. Most folks don't need your advice anyway. If we do, we'll invite it. Most folks like to find out our solutions. We'd like you to concentrate and help us do this. Somewhere way down the road, if you're bursting with an excellent solution, at least get the speaker's permission. Ask "Would you care to hear my ideas?"

## Step 6: Wait for the speaker to pause before asking your questions for clarity.

When you don't comprehend something, of course, you ought to ask the speaker to explain it to you. But instead of interrupting, wait until the speaker pauses. Then say something like this, "Back up a second. I didn't understand what you just said."

### Step 7: Ask questions that only facilitates understanding.

When you notice that your question has led the speaker astray, take responsibility for getting the conversation back on target by saying something like "It was great to listen to you, but tell me more about your adventure."

### Step 8: Attempt to feel what the speaker is feeling.

If you're feeling sad when the person with whom you are talking to expresses sadness, joyful when she expresses joy, fearful when she describes her fears—and convey those feelings through your facial expressions and words—then your effectiveness as a listener is assured. Empathy is the heart and soul of excellent listening.

To experience empathy, you've got to place yourself within the other person's place and permit yourself to feel what she feels at that moment. This is often not a simple thing to do. It takes energy and concentration. But it's a generous and helpful thing to do, and it facilitates communication as nothing else does.

### Step 9: Give the speaker regular feedback.

Show that you simply understand where the speaker is coming from by reflecting on the speaker's feelings. "You must be thrilled!" "What a terrible ordeal for you." "I can see that you simply are confused." If the speaker's feelings are hidden or unclear, then occasionally paraphrase the content of the message, or simply nod and show your understanding through appropriate facial expressions and an occasional well-timed *hmmm* or *uh-huh*.

The idea is to offer the speaker some proof that you simply are listening, that you're following her train of thought, not indulging in your fantasies while she talks.

In some situations, whether at work or at home, always restate instructions and messages to make sure you understand correctly.

## Step 10: Concentrate to get what isn't said—the nonverbal cues.

If you exclude email, the bulk of direct communication is perhaps nonverbal. We collect a great deal of information about one another without saying a word. Even over the phone, you'll learn a lot about people from the tone and pace of her voice than from anything being said. It doesn't matter what you are talking about; if you hear a tone of laughter in their voice, you can be reassured that they are doing well.

Face to face with an individual, you'll detect enthusiasm, boredom, or irritation very quickly within the expression round the eyes, the set of the mouth, and the slope of the shoulders. These are clues you cannot ignore. When listening, remember that words convey only a fraction of the message.

# Attitude: The Bedrock

Attitude is the manner, disposition, feeling, and position about a person or thing, tendency, or orientation, especially in mind.

It is a way you feel or act toward a person, thing, or situation. It is the position or posture assumed by the body in connection with an action, feeling, mood, etc.

Attitude can also be defined as a predisposed state of mind. While we use the word about how we think, it's related to the notion of posture. In the similar way that the body has a natural standing, so, too, does every one of us has a settled way in which we reason about things.

While attitude builds over time through a mixture of personality, history, and experiences, in the end, it is a personal choice. You can either have a pleasant day or a hurtful day; it's your choice. While there are exceptions, the general notion is true. Our attitudes are things we decide.

In marriage, attitude defines way more than any outward circumstances.

There is a popular saying that attitude is everything, and truly, sometimes it can sound like a bit of a cliché. We hear you! But in truth, attitude does make all the difference in the whole world.

If you entertain feelings of resentment, anger, or animosity against your partner, it's much difficult for your marriage to be successful.

Consider it this way: If you had a friend who consistently nagged you or put you down, you would not want to be close to that person as much. On the other hand, if you had a friend who was always happy to see you and was in full support of you, you'd love being close to that individual, right?

The same is true of your spouse. If you foster a positive attitude toward your partner, your relationship will be more intimate, more honest, and more nurturing for the two of you. Your marriage will turn to a place you want to resort to, a space of warmth and support for both of you.

## *Look for the good in your partner*

They say "familiarity breeds contempt," and honestly, sometimes it's true in marriage. When you've been with someone for some time, it's all too easy to focus on all the things they have done that annoy you. That feeling like you'll shout aloud if you have to pick up one more dirty sock or balance the budget again after one more impulse spend. Most married people experience that from time to time in marriage!

Instead of concentrating on what frustrates you about your spouse, try to look out for what you love about them. Make a deliberate decision to notice all the good things you love about your spouse. If they have a great sense of humor or always gives you support in your dreams, acknowledge that. Enjoy the fantastic meals they prepare or the way they're great with the kids' homework.

Let your partner know what you love about him or her too. A surprise text or cute note hidden into their lunch will cause them to smile and remind them that they're cherished and valued.

## *Focus and dwell more on gratitude*

Gratitude is sometimes thrown aside when life gets busy or has more pressure. It's hard to recall to be grateful for your spouse when the bills are piling up, work is on overload, and the kitchen looks like a tornado slammed through it. You're concentrating on all the things that need to be done.

Train yourself to search for things to be thankful for about your spouse. If they take a moment to prepare for you a cup of coffee, cook dinner, or sweep the floor, notice it. Take note of their contribution to everyday chores like disposing the trash or balancing the budget for the family always.

Being grateful to your spouse can have a strong positive effect on them. Even more, tell them about it! Ensure they know how much you are grateful to them.

## *Celebrate every little (and big) thing*

Celebrating together is a beautiful way to get you both focused on what is good in your marriage. Do not wait to celebrate only the big things like a promotion, baby, or new home (although those things call for celebration also, of course).

Find time to notice all the little good things that happen in the normal course of the week or the month. Probably, one of you got some good feedback at work. Maybe you discovered the perfect gardening tutorial on the internet, and now your garden looks amazing. Or perhaps it's as simple as discovering a great pasta recipe on the internet!

We're so good at looking for problems in life and omitting the good things. Make it your business to search for all the good things, no matter how little, that are happening all the time. Then bring out your favorite beverage or make your special meal and celebrate them with your spouse.

You can also get into the shared habit of listing three good things about your partner every day before you go to sleep at night.

It may sound simple, but practicing positivity and gratitude is a powerful way to help your marriage succeed.

It is also important for us to take note of some attitudes that are capable of tearing the home apart, those are what I refer to as toxic attitudes.

## Toxic Attitudes

Toxic attitude, most times, are reflected when selfishness becomes the order of the day. When a partner begins to think of himself alone without considering his spouse, the resultant attitude is toxic. Let us briefly look at some of those statements that reflect a toxic attitude.

1. "You are supposed to make me happy." Marriage should add to our happiness, but our spouse isn't in charge of our joy. General happiness with life and self is something we should bring into a marriage instead of something we will get from it. When you expect your partner to make you happy, you are expecting from them something they can never produce. You should be the one to bring your happiness to the marriage.

2. "Because other people have hurt me, I can't trust you." Trust is earned, but when you say "I do" to someone, it means they have earned that trust. While they should continue to be trustworthy, spouses shouldn't hold their husband or wife responsible for a pain caused by somebody else. When underserved distrust is in place, it makes the marriage weak.

3. "I don't have enough." There is nothing wrong with desiring more as long as the desire doesn't stop you from feeling gratitude for what you already have. Some couples cannot appreciate one another because they live in a progressive state of lack. Never satisfied, they struggle with continual dissatisfaction. Those who can continue to contend for more while also having a deep sense of gratitude for what they already have, create the best marriages ever.

4. "What I do doesn't matter." We don't control every area of our lives, but we have far more control than we think. Owning what we should own strengthens us and others. When we fail to find out how much influence we have concerning who we are and what we do, it inhibits our ability to connect with other people.

5. "I deserve _____." We truly deserve some things in a relationship; nevertheless, when entitlement overrules, a couple is in a dangerous spot. By feeling entitled, a spouse will cease from working and will start expecting to simply have things given to them.

6. "It's not my fault." Defensiveness crashes connection and productivity. When a partner settles on an attitude of defensiveness where all criticisms are either meant to be personal or are received as a personal injury, the couple can never improve anything. They are prone to be stuck with problems because healthy communication can't take place.

7. "Life isn't supposed to be fun." There indeed is more to life than just fun, but enjoyment is an important aspect of the lives we've been given by God. When we don't seek playfulness and fun, the relationship can lose its freshness. While some individuals are more serious than others, all healthy relationships should include enjoyment, laughter, playfulness, and fun.

8. "It's better to get than to give." A healthy marriage is all about mutual sacrifice and submission. In a great relationship, the couple progressively seeks the well-being of the other. With both of them pursuing this path, no one is taken advantage of or being overrun. When this is not the attitude, an individual begins to make the relationship about themselves. They believe getting is better than giving, so they continually seek things for themselves at the expense of their spouse. The relationship becomes one-sided and not fruitful.

9. "I'm just so tired." Tiredness, as a temporary condition, is part of life, but some people have an attitude of weariness. They are always tired. Either because they don't know how to rest, they haven't

built endurance, or they find pleasure in the attention that comes through saying they are weary, they live in a continual state of exhaustion. This condition prevents healthy connections with others.

# Character

Character

Doing the right thing when no
one is looking

-CJ Watts

The character of a person or place involves all the qualities they have that make them distinct from other people or places.

For many young women, marriage is not even on the radar until high school and college are done and their career is underway. So why would they think about it now? Though marriage can be a long way down the road (if it's the will of

God for you), it can be one of the most satisfying relationships of your life. But it may also be the most challenging relationship you will ever face in life.

In a world where God's prescription of marriage has been challenged, we need to approach marriage deliberately. Too often, the world of weddings covers our view of what it truly means. When that view is joined with a lack of emotional and spiritual readiness, some young brides find post-honeymoon marriage a disappointing reality. Marriage is great and interesting, but you must work it out with courage. It takes sacrifice, commitment, and communication.

But while marriage is sometimes hard, it doesn't have to be frustrating. It is possible to prepare for marriage even as a single person—and in doing so, prevent much of the heartache other couples experience. Let me also take this pause to point out to us some characteristics or qualities applicable to every relationship but essential to a God-centered marriage.

According to the scriptures, "Love is patient and kind" (1 Corinthians 13:1).

1. Patience

   It is something that is very fundamental as one of the virtues Paul used to describe love as the virtue of patience. Marriage needs a willingness to listen, to put another individual before yourself, and to bear with your partner as they grow and transform. All of these actions need patience! This is why to foster patience in your single years—as you wait to connect the person God has prepared for you—is an awesome way to prepare for marriage. It may not feel good while you're single, but you can be rest assured that your heart is being trained in a virtue you will use daily in your marriage relationship.

The trials of marriage can be overcome with patience.

2. Kindness

Paul first described love to be "patient," then included "kind." It sounds so simple. Shouldn't kindness occur naturally when you are in love with someone? Still as anyone with siblings or a roommate can confirm, living in close quarters with another individual is bound to result in argument at some point. During those resentful moments, we have to decide to embrace kindness by considering the other person first before ourselves. This action will maintain and support your marriage if you've engaged in it while you are single. In Jesus Christ, we've got the perfect example of kindness to follow after. Our Lord Jesus Christ loves us so much that while we were still sinners, He gave His life for us. In the multitude of our disobedience and unbecoming attitudes, He still loves and cares for us; that is a perfect example of kindness. You have to look far beyond yourself in order to show kindness.

3. Self-control

One among the fruits of the Spirit that Paul explained in Galatians 5:22 is "self-control." The Bible tells us, "For the fruit of the spirit is love, joy, peace, longsuffering, kindness, self-control. Against such there is no law." Controlling our actions and reactions can be difficult when we feel offended or upset. But self-control goes a longer way than managing our temper; it impacts every area of life.

There are three aspects in which self-control is important and necessary:

1.  The way we spend our time
2.  The way we spend our money
3.  The way we spend our emotions or feelings

Learning to control your time and money in a way that honors God not only benefits you as a person but also creates habits that will bless your partner. But just as we should control our money and plan our time, we must also learn to properly manage our emotions by committing them all to God and by choosing love at every opportunity.

4.  Show respect
    Love and respect are two virtues that are vital to building a long-lasting marriage relationship.
    Respect is what enables us to recognize people as individuals. It helps us recognize people as individuals, not as obstacles to our desires. Respect reverences the humanity of other individuals and recognizes their value. Respectful acts prove that a person values people in the same manner God does. An individual who values others when single will bring that attitude into marriage.

Trust is the adhesive of life. It's the most important ingredient in a communication that is effective. It's the foundational
principle that anchors all relationships. This is especially true
when it has to do with trust in marriage.

It is therefore important for us to delve deeper into the subject of trust as it is a vital component that makes for a successful marriage.

To start with, trust is to believe that someone is good and honest and will not harm you, or that something is safe and reliable

Trust is the adhesive of life. It's the most important ingredient in a communication that is effective. It's the foundational principle that anchors all relationships. This is especially true when it has to do with trust in marriage.

Trust is very vital; without it, maintaining a healthful marriage relationship will be difficult.

It's a word that gets thrown around, but few people take the time to define it. Trust is the assurance or belief that you have in somebody else. From that belief, you form a picture in your mind of that individual. Based on their behavior, they either prove right your initial, positive view or put up a negative one. Your capacity to trust in marriage is established in your relationship before entering your marriage and must continue to grow even after you have said "I do."

## Key Trust Areas in a Marriage That Is Healthy

1. Trust that you are a team, first of all.

    In many marriage ceremonies, the declaration "forsaking all others" is added. When you think of that vow, it means that you and your spouse became a family on the day you married and are a TEAM. You went from ME to WE! That implies making your marriage the priority. Yes—over self, over acquaintances and family, and children.

2. You must trust that you will be faithful.

    Trusting your spouse only to share their physical self with you is characteristic of marital faithfulness. Being faithful is not just secluded to your physical relationship. It also involves being trustworthy and sincere about how and with whom you are sharing your feelings, dreams, challenges, and goals with. You must spend your time. You must spend your money (and your debt rate).

3.  Trust that you will not consciously try to control or harm each other.

    An environment of safety and security must be present in a healthy marriage. Even in the middle of normal conflict, be intentional to care for, love, and respect your spouse. Choose words that inform, not cause harm on your partner.

4.  Trust that you love your spouse for who she is, not for what you can get from her.

    Your spouse needs to be loved for who they are on the inside not just how they look on the outside. Being assured that your partner would choose you again irrespective of any physical or financial changes only creates a stronger bond between you both.

5.  Trust that you will turn to each other, not against each other.

    In marriage, you will experience difficulties, sadness, and hurts. As you walk through the down times, depending on each other helps to lighten the burden.

    Knowing that your partner has your back provides a sense of security in a healthy and trusting marriage.

    There is no better experience than reaching out your hand to your spouse, and they reach back out to you.

Now that we have talked about ways to trust in a marriage, it's key to examine yourselves and the experiences that shaped the way you trust individually. Your trust picture becomes shaped by the experiences you have with friends, family, and coworkers.

Trust in an intimate relationship is anchored in feeling safe with another individual. Infidelity, lies, or broken promises can seriously damage the trust amid a husband and wife. That, nevertheless, does not necessarily imply that a marriage can't be redeemed. Although rebuilding trust can be hard when there is a notable breach, it is, in fact, possible only if both partners are actively involved in the process.

## Peace and Contentment Is Everything

Focus and staying alert is crucial for any relationship. It's usually common for the day to start without complications. However, it can bring unforeseen obstacles that will put one in a place of needing to think and not react. Here's an example.

She drives the car to a meeting that is approximately forty-five minutes from home on a Saturday. The car is parked and she goes into the meeting for about an hour and a half. The meeting is over and she goes to get back into the car to go home, but it will not start. She is thinking, is something wrong with the transmission because the sound was baffling. She is guessing because she knows nothing about cars other than putting gas into it and that it takes her from point A to point B.

Making about three attempts to start the car, it then comes to mind to get out and walk around the car. She finds that the right side is sitting up on bricks. Both tires are gone.

In disbelief, she then goes back into the building to make a report while being very nervous and unsure how to handle this unbelievable situation.

When she gets back to the car, it is being lifted by a tow truck driver onto a flatbed, and an officer of the law is present. The location of the vehicle is in a city that will only send an officer of the law if someone is hurt. Otherwise, you must go to the precinct to file a report.

She calls her husband to inform him of what has happened and that the car is being transported to a tow yard. While talking with her husband, the officer and the tow truck operator is insisting this is the better thing to do and it will not be a charge because the insurance will pick it up. Even though there had not been any conversation about insurance, they were adamant that it would be safe.

Her husband was insistent on having them release the vehicle and to leave it just where it was. There was a confusing and unnerving conversation among her, her husband, and the officer for approximately fifteen minutes. She wanted to do what the officer suggested because he is the law but was not sure if she should do what her husband was telling her to do.

Is taking the car to the tow yard the best thing to do or is leaving the vehicle in the parking lot the best thing to do? What would you do?

Many times, in a state of confusion, people lose focus and become perplexed with what is the right thing to do. It's the place of confusion that is the key point. Confusion is not of God, and the enemy is laughing while you're bewildered. It may seem obvious to some where others contemplate on how to handle nerve-racking situations.

The right thing to do was to listen to her husband. The order has to be correct. It's God first, then the spouse, and then whatever comes next. Her husband picked up a tire on the way, and he used the donut in the vehicle to get the car on the road.

It's a true story that reminds us how to have peace and contentment within our home and within our relationship. Trust is a major hang-up in marriages. Stepping out on faith with giving your spouse the full realm to make a solid decision when you feel you're being pulled is for the sake of a better marriage, as well as having an unspoken moment of belief in your spouse. I thank God every time I think about this story. Something as simple as listening to my husband and trusting him for the decision that he made has simply made my life easier. Who will you listen to?

It comes down to the allowing the Holy Spirit to direct your path. There will be no confusion when God is allowed into the equation to remedy the mix-up. Having a relationship with Him will give guidance even when a challenge presents itself.

## Picking up the Pieces

It may take a lot of time and effort to reestablish the sense of safety you require for a marriage to thrive and continue to develop. Recovery from the trauma that was caused by a break in the trust is where many partners who want to get back on track may have difficulties.

Research has shown that couples must discourse and act on the following five sticking points to effectively move past a breach of trust in the relationship. You must

- know the details
- release the anger

- show commitments
- rebuild trust
- rebuild the relationship

Whether you were the offender or the betrayed, to rebuild the trust in your marriage, both of you must renew your commitment to your marriage and to one another. Let us quickly examine these points in a more detailed way so as to draw more understanding.

## Know the details

Even in seemingly clear-cut events of betrayal, there are always two sides to it. The offending partner should be proactive and honest with information, in addition to giving clear answers to any questions from their offended partner.

This will give the betrayed party a more holistic understanding of the situation. What transpired, when, and where? What emotions or problems may have imparted to this situation? What were the mitigating incidence?

## Release the anger

Even minor breaches of trust can result to mental, emotional, and physical health issues. Partners may have difficulty sleeping or have reduced appetite. They may become irritable over slight things or be quick to incite a response.

While it can be tempting to cram all of the feelings and anger down, betrayed partners must tune in and reflect on all the emotions that they have. Consider the impact of your spouse's betrayal on you and others around.

Reflect on how life has been interrupted including reflecting on all the questions and fears that are now emerging. Let your partner know all these emotions.

Even the offending partner is advised to express any feelings of resentment and anger that they may have been harboring since before the incident.

## Show commitment

Both parties, particularly the betrayed, may be questioning their commitment to the relationship and wonder if the relationship is still the best for them or if it is even redeemable.

Acts of empathy—sharing your pain, frustration, and resentments, showing remorse and regret, and allowing space for the acknowledgment and validation of painful feelings—can be healing to the couple.

Building off of this, spelling out what both sides need from the relationship, can help give partners the understanding that proceeding with the relationship comes with clear expectations that each partner, in moving ahead, has agreed to perform.

Both parties must work to spell out what is required to stay committed and to make the relationship work and progress.

In communicating this, avoid making use of words that can incite conflict (example: must, never, always, should) in describing what you can see, expect, or desire from your spouse. On the contrary, choose words that aid open conversation and use non-blaming "I" statements. For instance, favor "I need to feel like a priority in your life" over "You never put me first in your life."

## Rebuilding Trust

Together, you must put up specific goals and a realistic period of time for getting your marriage back on track. Acknowledge that rebuilding trust takes time and requires the following:

- Decide to let go or to be forgiven. Make a conscious decision to love by endeavoring to let go of the past hurts. While achieving this goal fully may take quite some time, committing to it is what's important.
- Be open to self-growth and progressive development. You can't repair broken trust with only promises and words of forgiveness. The underlying reason for the betrayal needs to be identified, examined, and worked on by both spouses for the issues to stay dormant.
- Be aware of your innermost emotions and communicate your thoughts. Leaving one side to think about the situation or action that breached the trust is not going to solve the problem. Instead, it is important to openly talk about the details and express all feelings of anger and hurt.
- Truly desire for it to work. There is no ground in the process for lip service or more falsehood. Be honest about and sincere to your wishes.

Once the above points have been understood by both sides, talk openly about your ambitions and goals, and check in regularly to ensure you are really on track.

## *For the offender*

As the partner who compromised the relationship, it may be difficult or even painful to be reminded of your wrongs. Remember, though, that the steps above are essential to the process of remedy and recovery. As you carefully work on them, show that the mischievous behavior has become a thing of the past by changing your acts if you are the one who lied in your marriage, cheated, or breached the trust. That implies no more secrets, lies, infidelity, or anything of the sort. Be completely transparent, open, and forthcoming from this time forward.

Be honest and work hard to understand and tell why the bad behavior happened. Statements like "I don't know" don't instill confidence or help you get to the root of the problem.

Take responsibility for your behavior and decisions. Ask for forgiveness for the hurt you caused and avoid defensiveness, which will only increase the conflict or crisis. Justifying your action based on what your spouse is doing or has done in the time past will also yield no good result.

## *For the betrayed*

While moving forward depends a lot on what your spouse can show you, recall that the work that you do also have so many things to do with your potential success. As you move on, day by day, work on understanding why and what went wrong in the relationship before the betrayal happened. While this won't help you forget what took place, it may help you get some answers you require to move on.

Provide positive answers and reinforcement to help give your spouse consistent feedback on things that please you or make you happy once you have committed to giving your partner a second chance.

## For the couple

While there's individual work to do, remember to listen completely to one another. Remind each other that you deserve open and honest response to your questions concerning the betrayal.

## Rebuilding the relationship

Once couples have pledged to rebuilding trust, they must work on treating the relationship like it is a completely new one. Both sides must ask for what they need and not expect their partner to simply understand what it is they want.

Do not withhold trust in this fresh relationship even though it is with the same partner.

Withholding trust out of doubt or anger will prevent you from emotionally reconnecting with your partner. This keeps your relationship from moving forward healthily.

Instead, work toward rebuilding the connection by doing the work required in building trust and rebuilding a mutually-supportive connection. Agree about what a healthy relationship means to you both.

Some examples involve establishing date nights, working on a five-year, ten-year, and even up to twenty-year plan together, finding your love languages, and checking in with your spouse about how you feel the relationship is going on or if it is living up to your expectations.

Remember that all relationships need work. Even the closest of partners have to work very hard at renewing the spark while making effort to grow in the same direction together year after year.

## *Getting professional help*

You can put more effort on building a healthier, happier, and more sincere relationship if you address the issues highlighted above and if you hold onto the larger picture: that getting through this is only possible if you stay strong and be more committed to working on it together.

A relationship coach can help you with the procedure of the what, why, and how of what occurred to help you both make progress.

Both parties must be open to seeking advice to have a better understanding of the event that resulted to the breach of trust. But you may desire or need to seek individual coaching in addition to couples' coaching.

There are several forms of treatment for partners that are designed to reestablish trust, communication, and connection that can be especially helpful. Through continued work and other methods of treatment, you may even end up with a more solid marriage after going through such a crisis.

# *Focus Is Key*

Focus is defined as concentrating on something in particular. It is an act that means bringing into view.

It is giving a lot of attention to what you are doing so that you do not have an accident, make a mistake, or damage something.

Do you read through your friends' Facebook posts and conclude that your marriage and your family just don't measure up? Have you had a feeling of discontent settle into your spirit? It may be time to improve your marriage by improving your focus.

For instance, I decided to experiment—I logged into my Facebook page and categorized the first ten posts (minus ads and recipes). I realized it's just a few examples, but here are the categories.

- I'm married to the spouse of my dreams.
- I've had great success on a project I'm working on.
- My child is highly successful.
- My child said something cute.
- Here's a cute picture of my child.
- I'm looking for information about…
- My family had a happy experience.
- I'd like to provide you with some information.
- Here's a cute picture of my pet.
- Here's my recent life situation.

My purpose isn't to complain about Facebook. This type of sharing is the nature of Facebook. But if you're already feeling "less than" and seven out of ten posts highlight how well all your friends seem to be doing in their marriages and families, it's enough to throw you into a funk. What should you do?

## *Focus on what's true*

What you see and perceive to be true is probably not the whole story. When those friends talk themselves into the lie that they disagree with their spouse and other married couples don't, they will come up on the short end of an unfair, untrue comparison.

Seek and ask God for friends who are real enough to tell you the truth about themselves, their lives, and their marriage. Permit them to point out when your perceptions are off base. It helps to have at least one mature Christian friend you can take your difficult marriage questions to and who will give you a straight answer and sound guidance.

## Focus on what's good

When you are feeling down about your marriage, you can choose to focus on what your spouse did that they weren't supposed to do or what they didn't do that they should have done. If you rehearse it repeatedly in your head, you can work yourself up into a headache. I'm not recommending this.

Instead, lay the misdeeds aside and focus on what you are grateful for. Philippians 4:8 tells us exactly what to focus our thoughts on—qualities and achievements that are good, honorable, right, pure, lovely, of good repute, excellent, and praiseworthy. Try that as a guaranteed spirit-lifter when you feel your marriage, or your spouse isn't up to par.

The next time you're on Facebook and think everyone but you has talented toddlers, fancy houses, and exotic vacations, try focusing on what God has done for you—what's true and what's good about your spouse and your marriage. You may find that God has been taking care of you after all. See if your marriage doesn't experience an immediate improvement.

# Put God at the Center

It is the will of God that couples remain married for life. There is no room for divorce. The same God who is the author of marriage is the one who can strengthen it to last for life. Believe and trust in His ability, grow in His grace and love. Your marriage gets better when you get better.

Realize that in this book, we have taken time to explain the necessary steps that will help maintain the sustainability of your marriage, however, we must acknowledge the fact that it is God at the center of it all, working all things out after the counsel of His will.

Proverbs 21:31 made us to understand that "The horse is made ready for the day of battle, but victory is of the Lord." All the principles, protocols, dos and don'ts in marriage will not work if there is no supply of God's spirit. Exploits in marriage is purely a product of the strength that is supplied by the spirit of God. The Bible tells us, "That he would cause you to be strengthened with might by His spirit in the inner man" (Ephesians 3:16).

The journey of marriage is more spiritual than it is physical; therefore, the strength that is needed to sustain it must flow from the spirit. It is important for every couple to live from inside out, that is, to lean on the strength that flows from inside out.

All the virtues that have been highlighted above are spiritual virtues that our regenerated human spirits express.

No one can truly love if he does not know God who is the author of love. The ability to trust God for who He is and for what He says is the hallmark of spirituality, and that is faith.

The lifeline of every marriage is the word of God. It is the word of God that minister's faith and strength and reveals the love of God to us.

The Bible tells us, "For thou will keep him in perfect peace whose mind is stayed on thee because he has trusted in thee" (Isaiah 26:3).

You must learn to set your mind on the word of God because it is the word of God that ministers peace in marriage.

As a couple, you must cultivate the habit of studying the word of GOD together.

In order to excel in the battle of life and destiny as a couple, you must first find peace.

Learn to take the word of God as your present reality. You must find grace to believe the word of God irrespective of your present circumstances. Consistently renewing your mind to the word of God will help you to experience newness in your marriage.

Since the word of God cannot fail, any marriage that is built on the word of God cannot fail. Let the principles that guide your marriage take reference from the word of God. Teach and admonish each other in love and understanding. When you believe in the absoluteness of God's word, your faith is reactivated, and the power of God's spirit begins to work in you.

Worthy of note is that, as a couple, you must depend on the leading of the Holy Spirit.

As a new creation in Christ Jesus, someone who has accepted the lordship of Jesus Christ, you have received the gift of the Holy Spirit to teach and guide you into all truth.

The Scripture tells us that, "The ways of a man is not in himself, it is not in man to direct his own steps" (Jeremiah 10:23).

Let us realize at this point that the Holy Spirit is the spirit of God and that He knows all things both the past and the future.

Anyone who is guided by the spirit of God cannot miss it in marriage. The Bible tells us, "For as many as are led by the spirit of God, they are the sons of God" (Romans 8:14). If we learn to adhere and follow the instructions by the spirit, we are less liable to make mistakes.

Marriage is God's idea. As such, to be able to follow through, we must stick to God's precepts. Marriage must be worked out according to God's will, and the Holy Spirit is the one that reveals God's will to us. Our plans, our visions, our goals, our resolves, our choices, etc. must be divinely inspired. The Bible tells us, "But there is a spirit in, and the inspiration from the almighty gives him understanding" (Job 32:8).

At the core of the new man in Christ is the pulsating life of God, a life that is manifested in light. Those who have this light within will know their course through any approaching darkness and will find the way to a bright new day. The life of God flows from within, releasing the grace and the ability to create the realities you desire in your marriage. So you must live from inside out. The Bible tells us:

> And this I pray, that love may abound still more and more in knowledge and all discernment, that you may approve the things that are excellent, that you may be sincere and without offense till the day of Christ, being filled with the fruits of righteousness which are by Jesus Christ, to the glory of and praise of God. (Philippians 1:9-11)

Endeavor to bear the fruits of righteousness by the Holy Spirit and desire to see God glorified in your marriage. No one can be changed or transformed into a better person without acting on what he knows and believes. It is the doer of the work that is blessed indeed. Learn to act on God's word, putting to practice everything that you have learned from the Word.

Transformation comes not just by knowing what is right to do but acting on what is right. Don't just sit back. Go on and act on these things whether they are convenient or not. No success comes automatically; you must take deliberate steps to actualizing the success that you desire in your marriage. No one will do that for you, it is your responsibility to work on yourself, trusting in God's ability and wisdom to create the home of your dream. You don't need to wait for some time; start right now! Do something! Pick up your cell phone and place a call to your spouse, set up a plan for study, meditation, and prayer for your home. Start immediately to build up yourself for the great destiny that God has set for your marriage. Procrastination is an enemy to success; you must start now, not later.

Let me stress this point once again; live from inside out! Living means taking reference from your spirit which is the inward man where the life of God resides. The Bible tells us, "But to be spiritually minded is life and peace" (Romans 8:6).

You can only get better when you live from inside out. Your marriage gets better when you get better.

# Tools

Identify feelings. Communication is better when one can express how they feel. Example: "*When* _____ *was said, it made me feel* _____." Avoid the *You* word. "You made me feel this when *you* said this." It can cause defensiveness and a feeling of always being blamed.

*Happy*

Playful
Aroused
Cheeky
Content
Free
Joyful
Interested
Curious
Inquisitive
Proud
Successful
Confident
Accepted
Respected
Valued
Powerful
Courageous
Creative
Peaceful
Loving

Thankful
Trusting
Sensitive
Intimate
Optimistic
Hopeful
Inspired

## Surprised

Startled
Shocked
Dismayed
Confused
Disillusioned
Perplexed
Amazed
Astonished
Awe
Excited
Eager
Energetic

## Disgusted

Disapproving
Judgmental
Embarrassed
Disappointed
Appalled
Revolted
Awful
Nauseated

Detestable
Repelled
Horrified
Hesitant

## *Angry*

Let Down
Betrayed
Resentful
Humiliated
Disrespected
Ridiculed
Bitter
Indignant
Violated
Mad
Furious
Jealous
Aggressive
Provoked
Hostile
Frustrated
Infuriated
Annoyed
Distant
Withdrawn
Numb
Critical
Skeptical
Dismissive

## *Sad*

Lonely
Isolated
Abandoned
Vulnerable
Fragile
Victimized
Despair
Grief
Powerless
Guilty
Ashamed
Remorseful
Depressed
Empty
Inferior
Hurt
Disappointed
Embarrassed

## *Fearful*

Scared
Helpless
Frightened
Anxious
Overwhelmed
Worried
Insecure
Inadequate
Inferior
Weak

Worthless
Insignificant
Rejected
Excluded
Persecuted
Threatened
Nervous
Exposed

Beverly V. Thomas is a certified marriage coach whose life and experience have been a source of inspiration to thousands of couples.

She is a Christian, a wife, a mother, and a renowned author.

Through her experience, she has mentored many relationships and marriages. Her divine ability to reconcile broken marriages through godly counsel is worthy of note. After fourteen (14) years of divorce, she was reunited with her husband, and her marriage was restored.

Beverly's client says, "I truly enjoyed every minute of my time here. Ms. Beverly was professional and committed. I felt supported. I would recommend her to anyone who wants to work on themselves and their marriage. I loved most of all that God was at the head and in the center of it all. Phenomenal work! Words cannot express my gratitude. I found a rare gem in Ms. Beverly."

Through the lessons she has learned, the divine encounter, and inspiration from God, she has become one of the greatest marriage coaches. She is truly an instrument in God's hand to motivate, coach, and make marriages better.